# FLOOD

*by A F Harrold*

By the same author:

POETRY
*Logic & The Heart: Love Poems 1993–2003*

ENTERTAINMENTS
*Postcards From The Hedgehog*
*The Man Who Spent Years In The Bath*

FOR CHILDREN
*I Eat Squirrels*

First published in the UK in 2010 by

Two Rivers Press
35–39 London Street
Reading RG1 4PS
www.tworiverspress.com

Two Rivers Press is represented in the UK by Inpress Ltd.
and distributed by Central Books

Cover design: Pip Hall
Photo: Alex Cooke

Printed and bound by CPI Antony Rowe, Eastbourne

ISBN 978-1-901677-70-6

# Acknowledgements

Some poems have appeared elsewhere, sometimes in different forms or under different titles. *A Song To Food, On The Morning Sleeper* and *Watch* were first published in *Poetry London*; *Old Money* and *Driven* in *Boomslang*; *The Cloud Of Unknowing* in *The Interpreter's House* as *Poem*; *Slight, Artemis In The City, Suddenly It Snowed* and *Snow Arrives, Like Love, Overnight* in *The Nail*, *Snow Arrives, Like Love, Overnight* was also subsequently published in *The Oxford Magazine*; *Harold's Song* was first published in *The Unruly Sun*; *Love Poem* in *The Erotic Review*; *Atlanticism* in *Smiths Knoll*; *Keep On Keeping On* and *Bathing* in *Tears In The Fence*; *On Balance* in *Hand Luggage Only* (short-list anthology of the 2007 Open Poetry International Sonnet Competition); *This Englishman In Paris* in *Ukraine and Other Poems* from Leaf Books; and *Do A Little Dance For Me* first appeared as part of the on-line project *Like Starlings*.

Knots was commended in the 2005 *Bluechrome Poetry Competition*; *The Name* was commended in the 2006 *Salisbury House Competition*; and *Flood* was commended in the 2007 *Nottingham Poetry Society Competition*.

In addition, *Flood, Artemis In The City, Suddenly It Snowed* and *Snow Arrives, Like Love, Overnight* were published in the limited edition collection *Of Birds & Bees* (Quirkstandard's Alternative, 2008) with images by Jo Thomas.

The author would like to thank his friends, family, colleagues and critics for making this collection what it is, and also to acknowledge occasional funding from the Arts Council of England, South East, some of which was spent when some of these poems were written.

*For Tracy Tsirikos*

Now north and south and east and west
Those I love lie down to rest.
— W. H. Auden, *A Summer Night*

# Contents

Flood | 9
Watch | 10
Bathing| 11
The Weight Of The World | 12
A Song To Food | 13
Old Money | 15
Sketch: February 14th, 2008 | 16
Knots | 17
The Cloud Of Unknowing | 18
This Englishman In Paris | 19
The Name | 20
Seen From A Train | 21
Slight | 22
Little Night Sketch | 23

**Nine Death Poems**
I. Looking Up, Looking Back | 24
II. Scattered | 25
III. Song (472) | 26
IV. The Phone Number | 27
V. On Balance | 28
VI. The Curse | 29
VII. Song (607) | 30
VIII. Time-Bomb | 31
IX. Time Travellers Are Already Among Us | 32

Keep On Keeping On | *33*
Io | *35*
Suddenly It Snowed | *36*
The Poet Attempts the Industrial Revolution | *37*
Driven | *38*
Free For The Moment | *39*
Harold's Song | *40*
On Not Being Aegeus | *41*
Late Sketch | *42*

**Thirteen Love Poems**

I. Artemis In The City | *43*
II. To pause with partly opened lips | *44*
III. Snow Arrives, Like Love, Overnight | *45*
IV. Do A Little Dance For Me | *46*
V. Footprints | *47*
VI. Love Poem | *48*
VII. Good Enough To Eat | *49*
VIII. On The Morning Sleeper | *50*
IX. Notes | *51*
X. Constellated | *52*|
XI. Star | *53*
XII. Apple | *54*
XIII. Grace | *55*

Mole-Hill | *56*
Atlanticism | *57*
Letter from Ledbury Poetry Festival, July 6th 2007 | *58*

## Flood

And after the flood
do we hear of the fish
who took new turns in their new world,
suddenly grown borderless,
suddenly grown infinite, wide and strange,
who end their lives
washed up, gasping as the waters sink,
as the infinite turns out to be temporary,
as the world turns out to be more ordinary
than extraordinary,
gasping on someone's carpet,
in someone's front room,
gazing up with one fishy-eye
at the near sky, the ceiling,
the light bulb hanging close and bright
like a faint simulacrum of the sun?

## *Watch*

I own three watches (two belonged to dead men,
and one's all my own) and none of them work.
I looked, just now, and saw the time, read the hands
and thought how slow the day's going. Of course,
this watch is simply keeping its own grip on time,
on a time it much preferred to now: an hour ago
when the sun was lower, when the frost still blazed
and so much more future lay untouched, wide
and fresh to be discovered, like a lost rose-garden.

It's unhelpful, this nostalgia lodged in the clockwork:
it's tough on my appointments, tough on my being
where I said I'd be, just when I said I'd be there.
But, I suppose, were you to cut me open, lever apart
the parts of my brainpan to expose the grey,
you'd see (metaphysically thinking) the hands there
striking the same pose: paused an hour ago, a year ago,
or stuck even further back: childhood, perhaps,
or in the midst of some event which never happened.

# Bathing

Here's another view of that private pool, that daily grove
that's hidden from view by frosted glass, all steamed up:
I remembered it was there you first saw the naked me.

I didn't think it much of a crime, couldn't see the fuss
the prim old goddess made. I thought it all rather nice,
in fact, for being so unexpected, though I forget details.

It was the big bath at your flat, I remember that much.
I guess a woman has a right of way in her own bathroom:
no need for blushing or coy excuses to come and gander

at this half-submerged, recently captured bear, rotund
and hairy, in clear water, waiting patiently for pink salmon
to brush his paw. You never held with surfactants:

no foam, no bubbles – just glassy water all the way down,
like an open window. I couldn't hide a thing. Sleepily
I looked up and you were blurred without my glasses:

I couldn't tell where you looked. So I stopped the book
I held in my hands and we talked, like we did back then.
This memory is clear, like so few – I'm still there, now.

And later on, on other days, I remember you in the shower,
remember hurrying with you through rain, watching it
from train windows – see droplets chase droplets like kids –

but then this idiot brain, this grey sponge full of holes,
is rotten, shocks me with what it considers unimportant –
you see, it doesn't recall when it first saw the naked you.

## The Weight Of The World

That afternoon you rolled on the lawn,
flung your legs in the air,
balanced as best as you could,
your face, red, bent aside on the turf,
arms spread wide,
hands gripping the grass.

*Take the picture,*
*I can't hold this much longer.*

Later you twisted the photo round:
your feet rested on empty air,
as you shouldered that green ceiling of the Earth.

Zoom out, and there you are,
a tiny Atlas, lost to sight, underneath the globe,
everything above you, everything on you:
you, the lonely prop.

Ah! but see how easy it is
to simply turn the picture back round,
to evaporate that boulder,
unshoulder that burden
and turn ceiling back to ground.

# A Song To Food

*for MR*

There's very little in your fridge again,
and so we're going out to eat tonight.

I could grow used to this –
a life dedicated to the menu,
to running fingers down the lines
and learning the languages of the world, just so.
I'll smile at the misspelt English glosses
written by almost bilingual friends
of Vietnamese, Chinese, Moroccan restaurateurs.

After deliberation I'll plump, time and again,
for the meal I had last time, since it was good
and I'm too cowardly to risk disappointment
(although disappointment sometimes still arrives).

Each restaurant we add
adds a new dish to my catalogue.

Somewhere in the kitchen are men and women
performing marvels with foods I couldn't even name,
cutting, folding, searing, marinating in ways
I've never even read about in books.

Let me live a life
away from my own kitchen.

Let food be a mystery to me – its workings –
let me be un-Socratic in this, incurious,
but let me lie full and satisfied in its arms,

astonished that it still loves me, accepts me –
me who grows fat on its labour,
who asks no questions and makes no effort.

Come to me cheese, come bread,
come soup and meat and tea –
I grew lonely without you, I miss you so.

In fact, food, I'll come to you –
look this quiet waiter's handed me a menu –
dear food, patient food – we'll be together soon.

## *Old Money*

It's the end of the days abroad, when a hand
reaches into the forgotten, almost hidden place
and brings out those coins, familiar in a new way.
The Queen looks up at you, welcomes you back.

It happens at the airport or somewhere else.
You've forgotten the weight, the feel, and then
you find your keys have grown strange too.
What door will they open? Such a fresh place.

Sometimes it's the best thing about being away,
this return. As if you've spent a week under
a surgeon's knife, having new eyes and fingertips
emplaced: a soul brush up; a retimed pulse.

Do you recognise yourself by these low hills;
do you hear their echo quietly ask who you are?

## *Sketch: February 14th, 2008*

The frost has melted now and the pavements drip
like Victorian tenement walls. The sky hangs low,
a ripple of white-grey sheeting overhead,
not looking much like clouds, just like February.

The letterbox rattles –
British Gas and British Telecom both want me back,
though not like that. The bank has written too.
There's little news there, no: *Mr Harrold,*
*I was sat at my desk and happened to think of you,*
*hence this statement of account* – not even that much.

Last night, or the night before,
the fog froze in the air like powdered glass.

Turning around I could see the path I'd walked
marked out by empty space. I brushed the glitter
from my beard and my coat and popped it back
into the air with conscientious puffs of breath.

And today the bank and a handful of utilities
are the only ones who care enough to write to me.

## *Knots*

I find knots forming at parties now, between the drinks table
and the stairs, between the bladder, heart and spleen.

Tight little knots of past, like bubbles in a meniscus,
or the salesman's bundle of balloons, or like that dream

in which you meet that girl again, and live together,
and laugh and lie together still, as if the years between

that time and now had never passed, as if the argument,
the split, the break, those letters had simply been

stages on a journey coming home, that ended right.
It's all one reason why I'm only infrequently seen

out at parties now: the little knots of memory and people –
too sober to meet strangers, too drunk to let things be.

## The Cloud Of Unknowing

And only by not owning the pale, cold mobile phone
  can you remain in touch with the precise pleasures
of being stood up. Of waiting in utter ignorance. Alone.

It's all too easy standing in a foyer or bar or public place
  to slip a simple message out across the airwaves;
so easy stuck on a bus, a train, leaving late, to save face

with a waving SOS, a placatory explanatory non sequitur.
  But the man stood there out of touch, abandoned, bereft,
has such joy: is she dead? lost? running late? He sees her

in a myriad of places, wearing a host of former faces.
  It's happened again, he says. Half-anger, half-self-pity.
He blames himself. And then he's sure this blame is baseless.

Her watch runs slow. A flock of ambulances whistle past.
  Is this the right place? Right time? Did she mean today?
Did she say yes from shamed politeness. Did he even ask?

And where is love in this? Does it deserve to have a place?
  A bitter kernel spins in him. He reads the posters.
Again. Remembers things. All crimes begin to interlace.

And all evening he's an actor. The focus of attention.
  The ticket-tearers are impatient. The couples passing in
try not to look his way. When seated they'll not mention

his nonchalant leaning pose. His calm. His wounded smile.
  Inside the marvel of unknowing grows. He's mystic.
All futures are still open. He's sure he can wait a little while.

## *This Englishman In Paris*

Adrift, as it were, in the Metro of a foreign language –
underwater (scuba mask and flippers), surrounded
by reefs and startling flurries of fish and cave-mouths,
the whirling parasols of anemones and the incessant
upward flutter of spinning, swimming speech-bubbles –
I am freed from so many strokes of the pen.

Here, where it's all going on (urgently, lovingly,
noisily, frequently), all going on all around me;
here, I know equally that I'm no longer involved,
can't be expected to be involved, to overhear anything.
This tall, heavy Englishman, indelicate in the midst
of these words, can't step in without flattening,
breaking, embarrassing, scattering them away. So,

I keep quiet, just a rambler-voyeur, a diver-passer-by
among the lovely French train girls with mobile phones
and with newspapers that look so similar to mine.
Let them talk. I'm grown invisible and am good with it.
I don't know what's happening. Would that I could do
this simplifying trick in England and in English too.

## The Name

As I only have one language, so I only have one name.
It was handed me when my hands were too small
to discriminate between such things and I held on.

Unthinking, you let alternatives dart from your mouth,
all fine names I've no doubt, but not now, nor ever, mine.
I'll answer them just the same, as I'd nod to a Frenchman –

I so love this brain of yours that's grown butter-fingers
for something so simple, and after so long. I relax back
into the lengthening list of names that I'll answer to,

walk over to, listen to, sit down beside. Is it hope,
longing or charity that leads me to so many answers;
that encourages my embrace of so many possibilities?

Occasionally I'll forget which name out of names it is;
putting a finger to this mouth of yours, I hush the noise.

## Seen From A Train

A station called Stone:
somewhere outside Stoke.
A good name, I think.

I imagine ancient man,
pointing names to things,
began here: Tree, Sky,

Mud, Man, Rain, Stone.
Further from the source
names became less simple,

more specific: Greater,
Lesser; Upper, Lower;
East, West; -ham, -ton, -ing.

Though both sorts of names
have their appeal it's good
to see where it began,

where things were simplest,
where man started naming,
somewhere near Stone.

## Slight

*for KS*

Kate said she'd once kissed a man whose cock
curved in such a way she called it Crescent Moon.
He took this bold nomenclaturic act of love
in this way: as a blade intent on cutting off
that part which set him apart from other men:
his assured memory amongst her hazy nights.

I feel sorry for him, for his not being engaged
by poetry on the front line, here where we wrestle
to gain a grip on such epithets, where we sweat
to raise the physical and passing into megaliths
of lasting language before we slouch into sleep.

How sad it must be to miss out on such subtle
but essential gifts. There is so little else to share.

## Little Night Sketch

The lightbulb swings
on loose connections.

The room flickers on and off.

# Nine Death Poems

## I. *Looking Up, Looking Back*

It was summer, I was lying outside when,
binoculars in hand, I suddenly forgot
every constellation I'd learnt, I lost the lot –
mind blank as unmined slate – but then

a pair of stars, a flickering smudge of light
reminded me of your eyes, that look,
and below them was another star I took
to indicate that turn of nose – your nose –

and slowly, surprised by it, by all this,
I traced out your face – rudimentary, yes,
boxy and half built of wishful guesses –
then arms and legs, the pose exactly yours.

And that pattern there, I named – what else,
but after you? – and thought to make a note
of where and how it sat, but as I wrote –
sketched out the map to show – I realised,

remembered, how in myth people raised
into the sky – memorialised – are mostly dead.
I stopped. This naming act of love ran in my head –
memory resurged – my god, what had I said?

## II. Scattered

Your last act – a breath, and then a pause.

And I know pauses in the past have varied:
a second some of them, a minute others.

I would have waited. But now years and fire
have settled the issue; with another breath –

ashes on a forest wind, soon settling on earth.

## III. Song (472)

Turn around, look behind you,
is there anybody there?

Just a footstep, as a warning,
saying darkly *Please take care.*

## IV. The Phone Number

What great disgrace he took away, what secret shame,
I never knew. Only that, for one reason or another,
he was hardly mentioned, like someone else's cancer
or an over the limit phone-call we'd all rather forget.

In time I grew uneasy about this conspiracy to silence,
and I unfolded a scrap with a phone number on it
and knowing it felt so wrong picked up the receiver.

And there was that voice, so distant it seemed quiet,
so lost it seemed surprised to have been found again.
As if he'd been doing nothing in his years away he spoke,
and I only wish I'd made a note of his own precise words.

But then I woke up and in the bright summer's morning
lay with my head foggy on the pillow and remembered
that he was dead, not sent away, not abandoned, just dead..

## V. On Balance

Last night, in dreaming, death slackened its grip
and you were there again, not bringing a message,
not struggling with something urgent: just there.

And when I'd woken you stayed awhile in memory,
smiling like the Cheshire Cat, until out walking later
I found an orange fox laid out on a lay-by's kerb,
pale-tipped tail still. Externally unbroken it seemed
simply to be forgetting, moment to moment, to breathe.

A spot of bright theatre blood spilt beside the jaw.
As if we'd met once, dead open eyes locked with mine.

And I wondered whether this was the way that death
balanced his books: whether your one night back
could ever justify so still and such a senseless loss.

## VI. The Curse

Just think – one day he woke and realised:
no need to shave – not just today, but ever.
The badger and the lather left lying there.

And no need to cook, to eat, to defecate –
to do it all again, again. No longer a need
to find change for the bus, a new chain

for his bike, and the cold Swarfega after.
No phone to answer. No need to fill silence.
No desperate news pouring from the radio.

Oh, it suddenly got so simple, so easy –
nothing ground in gears: no grit, no sand –
the heart woke light and free and inessential.

But still (perhaps it's jealousy) I'd curse him
with all those pains – both tedium and grief –
and have him live again and see him breathe.

## VII. Poem (607)

It's a part of life,
as much as happiness
and easier to find.

In every passing car,
on every fire escape
and railway line.

It's impatient but it waits.

In waiting it may grow bored
and attempt to entertain itself.
It is not a good entertainer.

Inside houses it waits
at the foot of each set of stairs,
on the underside of each pillow.

## VIII. Time-Bomb

The surprise was absolute, unthought of, undreamt of
and yet beyond denial – sat there bright in its bag,
unopened from the day it was bought, receipt intact,
tucked at the bottom of the cupboard ready for clearing.

The month had passed as such months pass... eventually.
From the long dead days to this unimportant birthday:
a birthday I cared little for, but which he'd planned for,
knowing, I guess, this gift wouldn't pass hand to hand.

It was luck, random timing, casual chance, hopelessness
that led to my clearing that cupboard on that day –
it was *nothing better to do* and *no time like the present*
and *put off too long already* – only clothes, jumpers, shirts.

I'd mentioned it, this thing. He'd listened, bought it
and never said a word, but then the dead do this to us –
plant their time-bombs out there in the world, in here.
They tick days away, patient as anything, as everything.

Then *Oh, remember me?* they say, suddenly, from nowhere,
spilling into the light as cheesecloth spills into the dark,
an apport, a name overheard, a look, a book, a haircut,
a letter arriving too late from the bank – and I say *I do.*

## IX. *Time Travellers Are Already Among Us*

I see dead people – I see ghosts –
I see the movements and voices,
the looks, acts and decisions
of dead people almost every day.

They come up on those small screens,
clog the big screen of the cinema –
are on the wireless – captured,
replaying lives, re-saying lines –

going through it all again and again,
until their business is finished
once and for all, perhaps –
songs sung by dead people, too.

And my bookcases are clogged up
with ghostly voices on each page –
the past talking into the future,
whispering, but without listening

to hear whether it's being listened to.
Even the dead who aren't yet dead –
still their voices echo out the past,
ring round my flat, through my head –

hear this, see that – and I swear
this must be the best of worlds,
as Leibniz still says – since we must know
one another so terribly well by now.

## Keep On Keeping On

Pass through the portal, the passage, the doorway,
the alley, the wormhole, the window, the chink,
the keyhole, the skylight, the gateway, the tunnel,
the pinhole that's forced in the butterfly's back,
crack in the rock-face, the cave-mouth, the well-mouth,
the trapdoor, the hatchway, the fanlight, the frame,
the eye of the needle, eye of the hurricane,
the hole in the ear where an earring's just been.

*But remember Orpheus, remember Eurydice,*
*remember Lot and remember Lot's wife,*
*keep an eye on the light at the end of the dark,*
*just keep keeping on and it might be alright.*

Slip through the eyelet, the loop of the shoelace,
the hole in the Polo, the witch-stone, the ring,
the paper-chain circlet, the ring of red roses,
the thumb and fore-finger of a diver's 'okay',
the hole in the pocket, the wallet, the handbag,
the hole in the bucket, the doughnut's one eye,
dart down the mouse-hole, the plughole, the pipeline,
through porthole or portico, triumphal archway.

*But remember Orpheus, remember Eurydice,*
*remember Lot and remember Lot's wife,*
*keep an eye on the light at the end of the dark,*
*just keep keeping on and it might be alright.*

Loop-the-loop smoke ring blown from a mouth-hole
and dive through the hoop (avoiding the flames),
go on through the silence that lives between words,
go on through the dark that's the gap between days,
live through the blink that cuts this from that moment,
and live through the adverts that break up the shows.
Pass through all intervals, set changes, quick changes,
house moves, bereavements and chapters of books.

*But remember Orpheus, remember Eurydice,*
*remember Lot and remember Lot's wife,*
*keep an eye on the light at the end of all tunnels,*
*just keep keeping on and it might be alright.*

## Io

Spending time at this window I see immediately
the house opposite, the roof of the bungalow next to it
and between them trees, a field and beyond the green,
more houses. It's a harmless view (calm, urbane),
always the same – just browner in autumn, winter.
Beyond it all blue hills rise behind essential pylons.

I think of the corresponding view on far off Io
(the most volcanic body in this cold solar system)
speeding round its parent, spurting sulphurous plumes
into space. It's there right now, hurtling and spewing,
pumped like a stress ball by Jovian tidal forces –
the landscape changing minute by minute as lava

pools, puddles and streams. It's not a quiet place.
As it spins, lunatic on the edge of exploding, I listen
for the ping of the microwave, hope my milk's not
boiled over the edge, formed a mat of thick skin.
This is my quart of violence for the day. Later
it will rain and the view out there will grow grey,

but somewhere I'm not looking, or can't see, I know
there are still bright things, terrifying things going on.

## Suddenly It Snowed

Walking home from another disappointment
along the streetlight lit streets, breath misting
occasionally, when, suddenly, it started snowing.

Fat sparks of snow were suddenly flood-lit
in car headlights – snow just there, just falling.
And it appeared in shafts where light spilt
from pub windows, from shop windows.
Falling, floating; shifting sideways. White.

Against all other backgrounds, in the dark
nothing showed, but there, in these man-made
shafts of light, that night, suddenly it snowed.

## The Poet Attempts The Industrial Revolution

It's the same music day after day. From my study wafts
the un-pitched percussive pit-pat-pat of the keyboard.
Any passer-by would be forgiven for thinking I'm working –

paragraphs rolling like ticker-tape, poems bursting into the air,
on wings, on springs, singing themselves awake and alive.
It's a nice noise, it sounds busy, but I don't like passers-by.

Like the piano-learner in the high-rise inner-city apartment,
all plasterboard walls, playing the floorboard keyboard
(old painted ivory, old painted ebony); playing practise drums

on cardboard; exercising tap-dance barefoot on carpet;
we're all just put-upon autodidacts trying to do our thing,
quietly. (Without causing trouble, without being noticed.)

In time man learnt to read in silence: lips still moving though,
mouthing the words' shapes above the clattering loom;
timing the turn of the page inside the warp-and-woofing.

Oh, you beautiful revolution, that brought us together,
squeezed in these cities, cheek-by-jowling one another;
oh, you beautiful work ethic, you who'll griddle the guilt

if my fingers droop, stop, ever step off the treadmill keys.
If I had a Smith Corona now, I'd have fingers like biceps.
Instead I have words and things that are like words ill-born

where the fat fingers hit enthusiastically the wrong buttons.
I'll never know what they would've been, mis-spelt beyond
comprehension. But the passers-by have their own opinions.

## Driven

*for CS*

It might have something to do with windows, my not driving,
something to do with the cliff-side lure of the squared frame
that simply seems to say *gaze through me.*

If the poet's not a lover of looking out or looking in,
if they're not a watcher, viewer, a glass-steaming, flat-nosed
note-taker then maybe it's time to jump ship, change jobs

and just get out of the business – buy some soft leather gloves,
an AA badge and apply for a licence: count how many men
salute you in an afternoon – what larks! But I'll be on the train,

or in the passenger seat, by the triple-glazed plane window
letting my fate rest in another's hands – I'm trusting like that,
and admiring too, of those who choose to steer,

who trust themselves enough to keep their eyes on the road
and their mind on the job, to not strike a passer-by, a cat
or lamppost as they cruise, glancing distracted momentarily.

## Free For The Moment

One day, walking from here to there in the rain,
I realised that I no longer carried that pain
that had been with me for years,
that had fed in the night on silences and spaces,
invaded all times, in all directions and all places.

As the rain seeped into my suit,
reaching in for the flesh,
I realised that I had not noticed the moment
that death had moved away
to seek other conversations with other poets
and that I was free for the moment
to look at the world
glinting, running in the rain.

Except my glasses were immobilised by raindrops
and I could see nothing
but the insides of a few things.

## *Harold's Song*

And on this night,
                              as you glance into heaven
expecting to see the flow and ebb of the Milky Way,
expecting the blue-white, red-white blinking of eternity,
expecting some sort of blessing sign,
you catch some second sight instead
only of the reflected light from the feathers,
shaft and head
                              of a plummeting arrow.

## On Not Being Aegeus

It's a black sail I see, but there's been worse news.
At least it travels slowly, sighs as the sun moves
and as the wind prevaricates on the waves.

It might be the ship sinks before the shore,
before sand sits firm beneath the butting prow.

Even now there's time for news to not arrive.
Let the sun set and then tomorrow we shall see
what survived the night; see if it was meant for me.

## Late Sketch

*for JK*

It's not so much you lose sight of the sky,
but that you gain sight of the ferns and firs,

the lindens with their warm green light, cool
and submarine. You catch a ladybird –

snared in between two quiet closing palms.

Let her go – let this small mercy drop

into the world. Let just one good act stand.
Away under the leaves she'll settle down,

forgetting deeply instantly the wrong –
the cage she'd found, those twice five fingers shut.

# Thirteen Love Poems

## *I. Artemis in the City*

It is not just in woods and forests
that I long to catch a glimpse
of that slim virgin bathing,

to see her small hands, rough
and slender stroke away
the mud from her face, her breasts.

Through tangles of traffic lights,
garden gates, parked cars,
between dustbins and staring cats

I expect her at any moment.
The world is beautiful at heart,
and I expect to be made to pay.

## II. *To pause with partly opened lips*

an inch, or less, above your cheek
where breath and those minute hairs
that spring from each square inch of skin
dance invisibly together
like a hovercraft will with sand or sea,
but silently and softly,
and how just one easy movement ends
this speechless moment's grace and turns
that gap, that pause, into a different thing.

## III. *Snow Arrives, Like Love, Overnight*

You go to bed some days under sharp pin-prick stars,
shrugging in the cold, but not expecting transfiguration,
and you pull apart the curtains next morning to find the world
transfigured: a new world – whiter, dazzling, simplified –

and you feel for a moment like the man who steps
out of Plato's cave, or who leaves the optician's shop
wearing new, clean glasses that stand you taller in yourself,
that make you notice the world is made of details,

or finally, like an Adam, who's got the opportunity
to point to everything he sees and give it all new names.

## IV. Do A Little Dance For Me

Yes, I can dance, the way a bear dances –
but not a hot plate under the feet dance,
not a goaded uncomprehending dance,
not a dance to rouse peasants' laughter,
but rather a real honey-dripping, trout-tickling,
harrumphing happy fat-bellied roar of a dance.

Spring's arriving and I shake the sleep
from my eyes, my joints, my limbs and brain,
step naked from the cave and let the wind
and sweeping sunlight sigh into my hair,
give one great breathy stretch and yawn and then –

like the buttoned-up shaman letting loose,
or like the loose-haired librarian after hours –
I'll start to dance with little rhythm, but great joy,
the way a bear might dance, when no one sees.

## V. Footprints

Look – here's a wet patch, still steaming
on the bathroom floor, where you stepped
fresh as a summer tide from the shower.

A footprint more impressive than Crusoe's
treasured sign, and more various: here's
another and another, diminishing in size,

diminishing in definition as they pad across
the hotel room to the bed, where you sit
towelling your hair, angry, still frowning

about the journey here, as if incompetences
of train managers and signallers were still
of any importance, when all I see is the silver

reflection of the light inside the outline
of this slowly drying footprint. It's yours,
my dear, step one, a sign – look, we're here.

## VI. Love Poem

Be my Circe, my witch,
transform me, send me down
grunting to the forest floor.

Watch my curly pink corkscrew
twirl to itself
as I ram my snout

into moist places, ditches,
in roots, snuffling
for the prize, for the wet truffle.

I'll live on all fours,
languageless, lazy, your prize pig,
a beauty bred for its meat.

## VII. Good Enough To Eat

I have the peace of cake.
I'm full, replete, stuffed
and, now, ready to sleep.

Feed me; I'm yours.
Pile my plate and love
is never far behind.

Love, a drowsy joy
perched between palate,
stomach and brain.

And seconds? Oh yes,
a special treat for those
who have already dined.

## VIII. On The Morning Sleeper

Naked you, sleeping in the morning light:
this early brightness that sweeps down
from ninety million miles away to say
it's time to face another day of endless stuff.

I envy you, shut eyes, snakes of black hair
flufferling in the breeze of your mouth,
hand under your cheek, breasts as sleepy
as the curve of thigh, as its dark shadow.

It's too bright, too late, too light for me, now:
morning's silent trumpets woke me up
and having risen I can only wait for you,
check the coffee machine is set, is primed.

## IX. *Notes*

A last kiss, for example, is more important than the first.
That first kiss is there for life, is set in time at its moment,
but every kiss thereafter is the last until the next occurs.

And each hug or wave goodbye,
however temporarily intended,
is just an aneurysm, slip, swerve, crash, betrayal

away from 'no more'. In a world of so many easy mistakes,
where even my memory proves to be less than permanent,
it's worth taking notes: only then, perhaps, I'll keep us safe.

## X. Constellated

I don't mean the true but hackneyed thing
about the heavier elements all being made
down in the hearts of early brief-lived stars
which burst apart and left the building blocks
for baryonic beings like you and me –

but rather I mean you're made of stars because
you choose to wear them tattooed on your skin,
and how I dream at night, and in the day
(when stars traditionally fade from sight),
of approaching like a pilgrim on his knees

who shuffles forwards over loose terrain,
to kiss the inked in stars like focus points.
And I'm not one for obeisance as a rule,
but from time to time things just add up right –
the stars and you have come for me tonight.

## XI. Star

The clouds are low tonight – no stars shine –
and I wonder if you, however far away you are,
might look up, and see something else:
maybe you'll tell me that even when I can't see them,
those tiny flecks of fusion still twinkle in your sky.

Perhaps you'll say that even when I don't think of you,
when days go by without my glancing at your picture,
writing you a letter, telling someone your name…
perhaps even then you still go about your business
as if the world didn't revolve around me.

## XII. Apple

In some other world
where physics turned out different,
where time's tug can be nudged
in either direction,
think how easy it is to say sorry –

pull back the apple, for instance,
unbitten from your lips,
reach up and hang it on the stalk
on the branch and with
one quick twist
leave it dangling there, untouched

as a fine light rain lifts off again.

## XIII. Grace

As hard as it might be to reach
  in and touch another heart –
to plunge a finger in the chest,
  to lever skin and ribs apart –
to angle through the stringiness,
  to fingertip the beating pulse,
to leave a mark that later on
  time might turn from true to false –

that fingerprint remains unique,
  in its time an honest touch –
the heart is just a piece of meat,
  an autonomic bloody pouch –
but still the metaphor stays rich,
  the centuries don't see it die –
and though we left our fingerprints
  and turned away – we didn't lie.

## Mole-Hill

*for SR*

Though you're a friend and nothing else to me
(as if friends were unimportant!) I still smile
with admiration at your landscape's curves –
like all curves, they make the world more interesting.

And when, through whatever rush you're in
or whatever draught goes by, that small eruption,
that swollen nipple thumbs two layers of cloth
to raise a fat pale mole-hill on your shirt,

I smile more, remember dad dead and how
grief was briefly allayed by sucking on a teat
like that, as if the rest of life flowed from it:
a brave, though futile, two-fingers up at death.

We've both seen so many ways of making love.
Let's talk of other things: this ... that ... the rest.

## Atlanticism

*for TT*

I have no way to measure the distance across
the Atlantic – all my books are shut, and besides,
I've long grown tired of finding out figures.
So while I know this side and that are sat

on plates that drift on whirls of fluid mantle
(meaning the sea's shrinking or growing that gap),
the top of my head won't tell me which way it goes.
It's unlikely, though, even if each minute

draws us together, that we'll be meeting thanks
to natural causes anytime this year.
And as the sun steps through my room, whitening
the wall and flashing on the computer screen,

I know its pale reflection glances down
at you asleep. And when in the end its beams
finally directly light your face,
touch your neck, your hair, I'll be spun

already off into the afternoon,
always ahead and powerless to toss
the future back for you to catch: no hints
to help you through this day still to come.

## *Letter from* Ledbury Poetry Festival, *July 6th 2007*

Think of it, Masha: I'm sitting right here
in a lecture on Auden, without you again.
Six thousand miles have kept you away,
or kept me away: it adds up to the same.

Auden, we learn, loved collaboration,
with Isherwood, Britten, Kallman, et al.
He was lonely, perhaps, but generous-hearted,
and relished this way of telling a pal

that he cared by sharing a task, a labour;
by giving a part of himself into trust.
Each act of creation shared with another's
a submissive act and not simply just

the making of something new and alive –
it's humbling, becoming and also erotic,
a chance to express what in conversation
is awkward, what in words is quixotic

and open to vapid misunderstandings.
How hard it can be to find easy words
that pin down exactly how much someone means
without sounding fey, or odd, or absurd...

it's cleaner all round just to get down to work,
and happier too. Two minds in one room
knuckling down to the matter in hand
and finding surprising new ways to do

or make the libretto or play that they want:
the compromise met and turned to advantage
delivers the goods from somewhere outside
the orchard or garden that either man's planted.

I'm reminded of you in the midst of this lecture,
of how we might shut ourselves off in your room
and there, without words, we'd work together
at practices no one could ever call new,

but which, in a manner other than speaking,
express certain truths as physical acts.
(Making love is, of course, a collaboration –
a breathless and laughing, enjoyable pact

made by two strangers who've met on the way
(we're always still strangers, no matter how near
we come to each other). Submission, acceptance,
engulfing, embracing, it soon becomes clear

inside one another, linked in that way,
that here's the erotic in all of its guises:
Eros v. Thanatos, Eros v. Logos,
and Eros who holds us and then analyzes

nothing at all.) I think back to that walk
on the beach when we planned out the novel I'd write
to make a quick buck, with a chateau and Comtesse
and lovers and secrets and a dark stormy night.

That thrill was the same (oh collaboration!),
the swift epexegesis, we walked hand in hand,
brains quick as loins sparking with ideas.
(I've still not yet written what we wrote on the sand.)

Now, Auden said life's experimenting out loud,
we're making it up and we're muddling through,
and those moments we find filling with grace
or with love or with awe are sacred and few

and as such are remembered and valued and cherished
and end up in poems: *A Summer Night*
by Wystan is one that's exploring this moment
(four friends in a field where Agape's light

fills them all up and in silence they lie –
Auden checked later that they felt it too).
And I think of the hazelnut Julian held
and then of the hall through which Bede's bird flew:

because, life is brief, but life's all that there is,
and we're maker and lover and keeper of all.
But this isn't new knowledge, isn't a newsflash,
what's novel instead is that here in the hall

is the son of the man to whom Auden addressed
the poem in question, he's here in the flesh –
it's something important, a link to the text,
a proof that the books and the world in fact mesh.

I saw Nabokov's son in this very same room,
eight years ago, read his father's work:
it's a filial space, with more than one ghost:
the dead and the absent both seem to lurk,

not darkly, not sourly, but just at the edges,
they hint at what's gone, and I don't forget.
My father's here too, as he often is.
Though dead for five years, the feeling I get's

that I've seen him more in these posthumous days,
that I've tried to live up, I've tried to be good,
tried to make something that might make him proud.
I think of his fingers, textured like wood

that did every job, that carried the lot,
and look at my lily-smooth digits and laugh –
I simply don't know what he'd make of this work,
this job that lets me spend days in the bath.

That's it with the dead – there's no way of knowing
their novel opinions from over the Styx.
(The messages seen to spew out like cheesecloth
from medium's mouths must somehow be tricks.)

And I think of you, Masha, while sat in this lecture,
with six thousand miles dividing us, yet,
your absence just sweetens the talk in this way –
I take a few notes down, try not to forget,

I pay more attention, I notice the light
change through the windows. The dust in the air
of this Quaker hall hired for poetry
spins as dust does, and I wish you were here.

I can't ask the dead to say how I'm doing,
I turn to the living for answers today –
so tell me, my friend, my missing one, Masha –
*ya lublu tebya* – am I doing okay?